Life of Solomon Bayley

A Narrative of Some Remarkable Incidents in the Life of Solomon Bayley,
Formerly a Slave in the State of Delaware, North America; Written by Himself,
and Published for His Benefit; to Which Are Prefixed, a Few Remarks by Robert Hurnard

By
Solomon Bayley
Preface
By
Robert Hurnard

A

NARRATIVE

OF SOME REMARKABLE INCIDENTS,

In the Life of

SOLOMON BAYLEY,

FORMERLY

A SLAVE,

IN THE STATE OF DELAWARE, NORTH AMERICA;

WRITTEN BY HIMSELF,

AND PUBLISHED FOR HIS BENEFIT;

TO WHICH ARE PREFIXED, A FEW REMARKS BY

ROBERT HURNARD.

"Persecuted, but not forsaken; cast down, but not destroyed."—
II. Cor. 4. 9.

Second Edition.

LONDON:
PRINTED FOR
HARVEY AND DARTON, GRACECHURCH STREET;
W. BAYNES & SON, PATERNOSTER ROW;
AND P. YOUNGMAN, WITHAM AND MALDON.

1825.

Life of Solomon Bayley

A Narrative of Some Remarkable Incidents in the Life of Solomon Bayley, Formerly a Slave in the State of Delaware, North America; Written by Himself, and Published for His Benefit; to Which Are Prefixed, a Few Remarks by Robert Hurnard

"Persecuted, but not forsaken; cast down, but not destroyed."—II Cor. v. 9.

Second Edition.

LARGE PRINT

LONDON
HARVEY AND DARTON, GRACECHURCH STREET;
W. BAYNES & SON, PATERNOSTER ROW;
AND P. YOUNGMAN, WITHAM AND MALDON.
1825.

PREPARED FOR PUBLICATION
BY
HISTORIC PUBLISHING

No part of this revised and edited publication may be reproduced, stored in a retrieval system, or transmitted, in any form, or by any means, electronic, mechanical, photocopying, recording, or otherwise, without the prior consent of the publisher.

ISBN: 978-1-946640-71-0

All Rights Reserved.
HISTORIC PUBLISHING
©2017

Life of Solomon Bayley

PREFACE.

IN presenting the following fragments to the attention of the public, it appears necessary to state the manner in which they came into my possession, and to give the reader a brief account of the Author, Solomon Bayley.

During the early part of my residence in America in the year 1820, I met with the piece containing the account of his escape from slavery, with the mental and bodily trials he underwent, resulting from that step: being much interested in the perusal of this simple and unadorned narrative, I was induced to make some inquiry into the character and circumstances of a man, the recital of whose sufferings and wrongs had deeply excited my sympathy. The information which, in consequence, I obtained from many respectable inhabitants of Wilmington, where I then resided, was in all respects gratifying, so far as related to his character; and was, besides, such as to induce a hope that his situation in life was about to become comparatively easy and independent.

    I learned that at one period of his life he had been instructed in the business of a cooper, and for some time had wrought at that trade; but feeling some scruples in his mind with regard to following an occupation which he believed had a tendency, though a remote one, to promote the sale and consumption of ardent spirits, he conscientiously forsook that employment, under the persuasion that the frequent and indiscriminate use of distilled spirituous liquors, had proved as injurious to the moral and religious growth of society, as it was admitted to be subversive of health, and the bane of domestic happiness. He then engaged himself as a laborer in husbandry; and while deriving his support from this employment, he one day happened to meet with the Governor of the State of Delaware; and believing it to be his duty to speak to him on the great responsibility of the station in which he was placed, and on the importance of a faithful occupation of the talents committed to his charge, the worthy Governor was so well pleased with his communication, that he shortly after promoted Solomon to the oversight of one of his farms, admitting him as a joint sharer with himself in the profits. This mode of farming, which requires great confidence on one side, and skill and industry on the other, is not uncommon in America; the landlord usually finding all the necessary implements and stocking the farm, and the tenant, the requisite labor to manage the concern. But I subsequently learned that he did not long enjoy the above mentioned situation, as the Governor was soon after removed by death. He then engaged himself in the employment of a person at Camden, where with his wife he now resides.--Solomon was moreover described to be estimable as a religious character, remarkably humble, patient of wrong, poor as to worldly possessions, but rich in faith and in many other Christian virtues: such was the account which was given me of this extraordinary man.

Feeling a strong inclination to see and converse with one, whom, from the description of his character, I already esteemed; I requested a friend who had known him many years, and whom he sometimes visited, to introduce me to his acquaintance, when he should next come to Wilmington; this he did, and on a more intimate knowledge obtained in subsequent interviews, the favorable sentiments I at first conceived of his integrity and worth, were fully and satisfactorily confirmed, heightened as they were, by his solid instructive conversation, and I may add, the just sense he appeared to entertain of divine things.

It was in some of these interviews, that among other circumstances of his life, he related the affecting account of the sale and purchase of his only son, whom he afterwards lost by death; he also mentioned several particulars of his two daughters, whom he had placed out in the service of respectable families, but who, on account of ill health, had returned home, and died within a short period of each other. While narrating in my family the particulars of these severe domestic bereavements, which he did with great feeling and sensibility, it was evident that he was no stranger to the source from whence true consolation is derived.

In common with my brethren of the same religious profession, and with many philanthropists of other persuasions, I had long felt a warm interest towards the descendants of Africa generally: but the peculiar regard which was awakened in my mind, towards this deserving individual, made me anxious to obtain more of his history, especially when I had a prospect of returning to my native country. I therefore determined to obtain from him as much of it as he should be free to communicate, and wrote to him two or three times on the subject. We lived fifty miles apart, and my avocations, as well as his, precluded our meeting again. I wished to possess it in his own simple, unvarnished style; but Solomon being a self-taught penman, and ignorant of orthography, though willing to oblige me if he could, made many objections on the ground of his incapacity and the advanced period of his life: he was, however, at length induced to comply with my request, and in a while forwarded me such parts as I had particularly requested.

I cannot but regret that the manuscript is so disjointed and incomplete, being written and forwarded to me at different times; but imperfect as it is, it appeared too interesting and valuable, to be restricted to the circle of my own acquaintance, and I offer it to a candid public, presuming that every indulgence on this score will be granted to a man, whose life has been chiefly spent in slavery and servitude.

Solomon is in connection with that body of Christians, called Methodists; and my last communication from him, sufficiently evinces on what grounds he has believed himself called to the ministry. From the general tenor of his writings, and from this letter in particular, I leave the serious reader to form his own judgment, whether he be not rightly called and qualified to be engaged in that important service.

I wish it to be understood, that it is intended to transmit the whole of the profits of the publication to

America, for the benefit of the aged couple; and I hope the friends of humanity generally, will, for this purpose, assist in promoting an extensive circulation of the tract; by so doing, they will also contribute to place SLAVERY in a new and appalling light.

This narrative discloses the melancholy and incontrovertible fact, that the rights of Slaves are shamefully invaded in a country, where a man is suffered to go unpunished, who has dared to sell and transport those, who are legally entitled to their freedom, by his own voluntary act: and if such be the case in America, notwithstanding all the vigilance of her abolition societies, it may be asked, what presumption have the friends of this injured people to hope, that any real benefit can result from the tardy and temporizing measures, which have been introduced into the British West India Colonies, where no public bodies are organized to take cognizance of their wrongs.

A period of nearly twenty years has elapsed, during which the friends of gradual manumission have been lulled by hope, and cheated by disappointed expectation; and when it is considered, that at this moment England retains nearly eight hundred thousand human beings, and America more than fifteen-hundred thousand, in this cruel state of bondage, it remains even now a doubt, whether the present generation will witness the end of this aggravated evil, unless prompt and more vigorous measures be taken for its immediate extinction.

R. HURNARD.

KELVEDON, ESSEX, 1ST MONTH 1825

NARRATIVE, &c.

SOLOMON BAYLEY, unto all people, and nations, and languages, grace be unto you, and peace from God our Father, and from the Lord Jesus Christ.

Having lived some months in continual expectation of death, I have felt uneasy in mind about leaving the world, without leaving behind me some account of the kindness and mercy of God towards me. But when I go to tell of his favours, I am struck with wonder at the exceeding riches of his grace. O! that all people would come to admire him for his goodness, and declare his wonders which he doth for the children of men. The Lord tried to leach me his fear when I was a little boy; but I delighted in vanity and foolishness, and went astray. But the Lord found out a way to overcome me, and to cause me to desire his favor, and his great help; and although I thought no one could be more unworthy of his favor, yet he did look on me, and pitied me in my great distress.

I was born a slave in the state of Delaware, and was one of those slaves that were carried out of Delaware into the state of Virginia; and the laws of Delaware did say, that slaves carried out of that state should be free; whereupon I moved to recover my freedom. I employed lawyers, and went to court two days, to have a suit brought to obtain my freedom. After court I went home to stay until the next court, which was about six weeks off. But two days before the court was to sit, I was taken up and put on board of a vessel out of Hunting Creek, bound to Richmond, on the western shore of Virginia, and there put into Richmond jail, and irons were put on me; and I was brought very low. In my distress I was often visited with some symptoms of distraction. At length I was taken out of jail, and put into one of the back country wagons, to go toward the going down of the sun. Now consider, how great my distress must have been, being carried from my wife and children, and from my natural place, and from my chance for freedom.

On the third day my distress was bitter, and I cried out in my heart, 'I am past all hope:' and the moment I said I was past all hope, it pleased the father of all mercy to look on me, and he sent a strengthening thought into my heart, which was this: that he that made the heavens and the earth, was able to deliver me. I looked up to the sky, and then to the trees and ground, and I believed in a moment, that if he could make all these, he was able to deliver me. Then did that scripture come into my mind, which I had heard before, and that was, "they that trust in the Lord, shall never be confounded." I believed that was a true word, and I wanted to try that word, and got out of the wagon; but I thought I was not fit to lay hold of the promise: yet another thought came into my mind, and that was, that I did not know to what bounds his mercy would extend. I then made haste and got out of the wagon, and went into the bushes; I squatted down to see what would follow. Now there were three wagons in company, and four white people; they soon missed me, and took out one of the horses and rode back, and were gone about three-quarters of an hour, and then returned, and put the horse in the wagon again, and went on their way; and that was the last I ever saw or heard of them. I sat still where I was till night, and then walked out into the road and looked up to the sky, and I felt very desolate. Oh! the bitterness of distress which I then felt, for having sinned against God; whom if I had been careful to obey in all things, he would have spared me all my troubles. Oh! it is a dangerous thing to cast off fear, and to restrain prayer before God. If we do that which we believe will please him, with a desire to obtain his favor, it is a real prayer; but if we do, or say, that which we believe will displease him, that is to cast off fear, and to restrain prayer before him.

When night came and I walked out of the bushes, I felt very awful. I set off to walk homewards, but soon was chased by dogs, at the same house where the man told the Waggoner he had taken up a runaway three days before. But it pleased the highest, to send out a dreadful wind, with thunder and lightning, and rain; which was the means by which I escaped, as I then thought, as I travelled along that night. Next day I was taken with the dysentery, which came on so bad, I thought I must die; but I obtained great favor, and kept on my feet, and so I got down to Richmond; but had liked to have been twice taken, for twice I was pursued by dogs.

But after I got to Richmond, a cultured man pretended to be my friend, and then sent white people to take me up; but a little while before they came, it came expressly into my mind, that he would prove treacherous and betray me. I obeyed the impression immediately, and left the place I was in, and presently there came with clubs to take me, as it did appear, two white men and a cultured man. When I saw them I was in an hollow place on the ground, not far from where the cultured man left me: at sight of them I was struck with horror and fear, and the fear that came into my soul, took such an impression on my animal frame, that I felt very weak: I cried to the Maker of heaven and earth to save me, and he did so. I lay there and prayed to the Lord, and broke persimmon tree bushes, and covered myself: when night came on, I felt as if the great God had heard my cry. Oh! how marvelous is his loving kindness toward men of every description and complexion. Though he is high, yet hath he respect unto the lowly, and will hear the cry of the distressed when they call upon him, and will make known his goodness and his power.

I lay there till night, and then with great fear I went into the town of Richmond, and enquired the way over the river to go to Petersburg, where I stayed near three weeks, in which time, severe and painful were my exercises: I appeared to be shut up in such a straight case, I could not see which way to take. I tried to pray to the Lord for several days together, that he would be pleased to open some way for me to get along. And I do remember, that when I was brought to the very lowest, suddenly a way appeared, and I believe it was in the ordering of a good providence.

It was so; there came a poor distressed cultured man to the same house where I had taken refuge: we both agreed to take a craft, and go down James' River, which was attended with great difficulty, for we met with strict examination twice, and narrowly escaped; we had like to have been drowned twice, once in the river, and once in the bay. But how unable were we to offer unto God that tribute of praise due to his name, for the miracle of grace shewn to us in our deliverance! Surely wisdom and might are his, and all them that walk in pride he is able to abase. Oh!

> "Let all the world fall down and know
> "That none but God such power can shew."

We got safe over to the eastern shore of the Chesapeake

Bay, where his wife and mine were. And now, reader, I do not tell thee how glad I was, but will leave thee to judge, by supposing it had been thy own case. We landed near Nandew, and then started for Hunting Creek, and we found both our wives; but we found little or no satisfaction, for we were hunted like partridges on the mountains.

My companion got to work on board of a vessel to get clams, perhaps to get some money to bring suit for his freedom, (as he had been sold like me, out of the state of Delaware,) if his master should come after him from the back countries, who he said, lived about three hundred and thirty miles from the eastern shore; but poor fellow, they went on board of the vessel where he had been at work, and talked of taking him up and putting him in jail, and of writing to his master in the back countries. He was said to tell them, that he had rather die than to be taken and carried away from his wife again: and it was said, they went down into the cabin and drank, and then came up on deck and seized him, and in the scuffle he slipped out of their hands, and jumped overboard, and tried to swim to an island that was not far off; but they got out the tow boat and went after him, and when they overtook him, he would dive to escape, and still he tried to reach the island: but they watched their opportunity as he rose, when they struck him with the loom of the oar, and knocked his brains out, and he died. And now, reader, consider if you had been carried away from your wife and children, and had got back again, how hard it would seem to be, to be thus chased out of the world; but the great God, whose eyes behold the things that are equal, he continues to make such repent, either in this world, or in the world to come, And now, readers, you have heard of the end of my fellow-sufferer, but I remain as yet, a monument of mercy, thrown up and down on life's tempestuous sea; sometimes feeling an earnest desire to go away and be at rest; but I travel on, in hopes of overcoming at my last combat.

But I will go on to tell of my difficulties. After I came over the bay, I went to see my wife, but was still in trouble; and it was thought best to leave the state of Virginia and go to Dover, and then if my master came after me, to bring suit at Dover, and have a trial for my freedom. The distance from where I then was to Dover, was about one hundred and twenty miles: so I started and travelled at nights, and lay by in the day time. I went on northwards, with great fear and anxiety of mind. It abode on my mind that I should meet with some difficulty before I got to Dover: however I tried to study on the promises of the Almighty, and so travelled on until I came to a place called Anderson's Cross-Roads; and there I met with the greatest trial I ever met with in all my distress. But the greater the trial, the greater the benefit, if the mind be but staid on that everlasting arm of power, whom the winds and the waves obey. It was so, that I called at them cross-roads, to enquire the way to Camden, and I thought I would go to the kitchen where the black people were; but when the door was opened, it was a white man I saw, of a portly appearance, with a sulky down look. Now the day was just a breaking: he raised up out of his bed, and came towards the door and began to examine me, and I did not know what to say to him; so he soon entangled me in my own talk, and said, I doubt you are a lying: I said I scorn to lie; but I felt very weak and scared, and soon bid him farewell and started. I went some distance along the road, and then went into the woods, and leaned my back against a tree to study, and soon fell to sleep; and when I waked, the sun was up, and I said to myself, if I stand sleeping about here, and that man that examined me in the morning comes to look for me and finds me, he may tie me before I get awake; for the poor fellow that came across the bay with me told me, that he travelled all night, and in the morning he met a cultured man, and passed on, and went into the woods and lay down, and went to sleep; and he said there came white men and tied him, and waked him up to go before the justice; but so it was, he got away from them and found me at Petersburg So considering on what he had told me, and that man's examining me in the morning, made me I did not know what to do. I concluded to look for a thick place and lay down, and then another thought came into my mind, and that was, to look for a thin place, and there lie down. So I concluded to do so; withal I thought to take a sally downwards, as I enquired of the man to go upwards, I thought by going a little downwards, would be a dodge, and so I should miss him: I thought this plan would do. I then looked for a thin place, and lay down and slept till about nine o'clock, and then waked; and when I awoke, I felt very strange: I said to myself I never felt so in all my distress: I said something was going to happen to me to-day.

So I studied about my feelings until I fell to sleep, and when I awoke, there had come two birds near to me; and seeing the little strange looking birds, it roused up all my senses; and a thought came quick into my mind that these birds were sent to caution me to be away out of this naked place; that there was danger at hand. And as I was about to start, it came into my mind with great energy and force, "if you move out of this circle this day, you will be taken;" for I saw the birds went all round me: I asked myself what this meant, and the impression grew stronger, that I must stay in the circle which the birds made. At the same time a sight of my faults came before me, and a scanty sight of the highness and holiness of the great Creator of all things. And now, reader, I will assure thee I was brought very low, and I earnestly asked what I should do: and while I waited to be instructed, my mind was guided back to the back countries, where I left the wagons about sixty or seventy miles from Richmond, towards the sun-setting; and a question arose in my mind, how I got along all that way, and to see if I could believe that the great God had helped me notwithstanding my vileness. I said in my heart, it must be the Lord, or I could not have got along, and the moment I believed in his help, it was confirmed in my mind, if he had begun to help me, and if he did send those birds, he would not let anything come into the circle the birds had made; I therefore tried to confirm myself in the promises of God, and concluded to stay in the circle; and so being weary, travelling all night, I soon fell to sleep; and when I awaked, it was by the noise of the same man that examined me in the morning, and another man, an old conjuror, for so I called him. And the way they waked me was by their walking in the leaves, and coming right towards me. I was then sitting on something about nine inches high from the ground, and when I opened my eyes and saw them right before me, and I in that naked place, and the sun a shining down on me about eleven o'clock, I was struck with dread, but was afraid to move hand or foot: I sat there, and looked right at them; and thought I, here they come right towards me; and the first thought that struck my mind was, am I a going to sit here until they come and lay hands on me? I knew not what to do; but so it was, there stood a large tree about eleven or twelve yards from me, and another big tree had fallen with the top limbs round it: and so it was, through divine goodness, they went the other side of the tree, and the tree that had fallen, was between them and me. Then I fell down flat upon my face, on the ground; as I raised up my head to look, I saw the actions of this old craftsman; he had a stick like a surveyor's rod; he went along following his stick very diligently. The young man that examined me in the morning, had a large club, with the big end downwards, and the small end in his hand; he looked first one side, and then on the other: the old man kept on away past me about sixty yards, and then stopped; and I heard him say, "he h'ant gone this way." Then he took his stick and threw it over his shoulder, and pointed this way and that way, until he got it right towards me; and then I heard him say, "come let us go this way." Then he turned his course and came right towards me: then I trembled, and cried in my heart to the Lord, and said, what shall I do? what shall I do? and it was impressed on my mind immediately, "Stand still and see the salvation of the Lord;" the word that was spoken to the children of Israel when at the Red Sea. And I said in my heart, bless the Lord, O my soul; I will try the Lord this time. Here they come; and still that word sounded in my heart; "Stand still and see the salvation of the Lord." They came not quite so near me as the circle the birds had made, when the old man sheared off, and went by me; but the young man stopped and looked right down on me, as I thought, and I looked right up into his eyes; and then he stood and looked right into my eyes, and when he turned away, he ran after the old man, and I thought he saw me; but when he overtook the old man, he kept on, and then I knew he had not seen me. Then I said, bless the Lord, he that gave sight to man's eyes, hath kept him from seeing me this day: I looked up among the trees and said, how dreadful is this place. I said, two great powers have met here this day; the power of darkness, and the power of God; and the power of God has overthrown the power of darkness for me a sinner. I thought I must jump and shout, but another thought struck my mind, that it was not a right time to shout; I therefore refrained. But my heart was overwhelmed at the sight of the goodness and power of God, and his gracious readiness to help the stranger in distress: though he is high, yet hath he respect unto the lowly. It is a solemn truth, he is nigh to all them that call on him, with a view to his greatness and their own nothingness: I felt greatly at loss to know how to adore him according to his excellent greatness. I said, has the maker of heaven and earth took my part? I said again, what could all the world do in comparison with him? I now believed if everybody in the world was engaged against me, that he was able to deliver me out of their hands.

After a while I moved out of that place, and went away to a small stream of water, and stayed there a little while, and then went out of that neighborhood. But whether I did right or not, I know not; for in moving out of that circle so quickly, I became so bewildered as to be quite lost, and did not know what course to take, or what to do; and I thought it was because my faith failed me so quickly. Oh! what pains God doth take to help his otherwise helpless creatures. O that his kindness and care were more considered and laid to heart, and then there would not be that cause to complain that "the ox knoweth his owner, and the ass his master's crib, but Israel doth not know, my people doth not consider." Oh! how marvelous is his loving-kindness toward people of every description, both high and low, rich and poor. O that all people would study to please him, for his goodness and his power; for his wisdom is great, and he knoweth how to deliver all those that look unto him, and will pass by none, no not the least of all his human creatures; and he will make them see that they are of more value than many sparrows; and that they are not their own, but that they are bought with a price.

Now unto the king immortal, invisible, the only wise God, be glory and honor, dominion and power, now and forever. Amen.

After this, my understanding was opened to see for what purpose this last trial had happened unto me; and it was impressed on my mind that I had come through difficulties and troubles, in order that my faith and confidence might be tried; and that I might be made strong in the faith to believe that so high and holy an one, who had thus marvelously preserved me, would hereafter help so poor an object as me, out of his great mercy and condescension, and that I might be afraid again to sin against his majesty, who had suffered me to be thus sorely tried, that I might see the greatness of my past transgressions, and his boundless loving-kindness and mercy.

END OF PART I.

SECOND PART.

What follows, was written and communicated to me at my request, but without any idea on the part of the writer, of the purpose to which I designed it; the originals of which, if desired, may be seen by application to me, in order to satisfy any who might feel a doubt with regard to the faithfulness of the transcript. I can, however, assure the reader, that the alterations I have ventured to make, have been almost altogether confined to the spelling.--R. H.]

7th Mo. 24, 1799, I got to Camden. I will yet go on to shew the reader my uneasiness of mind after I got to Camden. I then thought I wanted a preparation to adore the goodness of God, that had begun with the me in the back countries, and had brought me through so many difficulties; but with shame I must confess, I sang his praise, but soon forgot his works: yet the great God pitied me, and exercised a careful constant mind towards me, for my good: Oh! how deceitful is the heart of man.

But not long after I got to Camden, my master came from the state of Virginia, to Camden, Kent County, state of Delaware, where he found me; whereas he had not seen me since he put me aboard of the back country wagon, which, as I suppose, is near three or four hundred miles from Camden: upon first sight he asked me what I was a going to do? I says, how, master? he asked me, how did I think I was a going to get free, by running and dodging about in that manner? I said, why, master, I have suffered a great deal, and seen a great deal of trouble, I think you might let me go for little or nothing: he said, I won't do that, but I will give you the same chance I gave you before I sent you away; give me forty pounds bond and security, and you may be free: but I replied, I work hard at nights to get a little money to fee my lawyers, and if it had been right for me to be free, I ought to have been free without so much trouble; he asked me who I blamed for my trouble? I answered, I did not consider that I was to blame: Ah! said he, you can see other people's faults, but cannot see your own. I said, master, you can't blame me for a thing I never did; Ah! said he, my wrongs don't make your's right, and that word put me to silence; but I thought where the laws of the land made liberty the right of any man, he could not be wrong in trying to recover it: but finally he sold me my time for eighty dollars and I dropped the lawsuit. I went to work, and worked it out in a shorter time than he gave me, and then I was free from man.

  And when I came to think that the yoke was off my neck, and how it was taken off, I was made to wonder, and to admire, and to adore the order of kind providence, which assisted me in all the way. But I found in me a disposition to wander from the path of life, and forget the favor bestowed upon me, and went astray too shameful to be mentioned.

But in this lost condition there came a reasoning to me, to consider where I was a going, and where I should end; and to consider on the shortness of time, and the length of eternity: and a thought came into my mind, assuring me that my life was in the hand of God, and that he was looking for better behavior from me; and that he was angry with me every day; and that he had whetted his sword, and made ready his arrows to shoot at me. Then my understanding began to be enlightened, to see my dreadful state by nature; and the more I considered on the nature and heinousness of my sin, both in thought, word, and deed, the more I was distressed in mind; but I found the sentence of death was passed against me, and it pressed on my mind, if I kept on going against light, I should soon feel the heat of the burning lake, or the misery of those that are driven to darkness at death. And when I considered the power of God, and for that power to be poured out upon me to all eternity, I began then to examine into my state and condition, and I found I had a falling spirit, prone to evil as the sparks fly upward; then I set myself to think how I could escape the misery that was coming on me. I considered my punishment would be as bad as those that went to darkness in old time: then I began to consider what God had done to save mankind from that fearful condition; and while I thought on the many ways he had taken to shew his earnest mind to save sinners, this consideration moderated my distress; but when I remembered my own ways that were not good, I felt ashamed even to lift my eyes to heaven to ask pardon for my sins; but the shortness of time, and the length of awful eternity, so arrested my mind, that I was made to realize eternal misery, and to cry like Jonah, as out of the belly of hell, for mercy and for pardon for all my sins. Oh! the thought of being amongst that black crew, when the Lord rains down snares, fire, and brimstone, and horribleness, terrified me much.

And now, reader, I will here record that God is rich in mercy, towards sinners of the deepest die; for when every other method failed, to shew his steadfast mind to save me, he sent a little boy to me with his finger at a text in a sermon book, "The wicked is driven away in his wickedness, but the righteous hath hope in his death; the same text I had heard a Methodist preacher take on a funeral occasion; then that little boy coming to me with his finger pointing at the same in the sermon book, it was about noon, the people nearly all gone to meeting, and I reading very earnest in the Testament: I took the book and began to read, and it pleased infinite goodness to look on me from the throne of his highness, and being unwilling that I should perish eternally, he sent down his awakening power, and I was made to quake and tremble; and an impression abode on my mind, that God was a true, and a just, and a holy God, and that no unclean thing could rest in his holy habitation. I saw I was a sinner condemned to die, but a call reached my soul, "take heed that you entertain no hopes of heaven, but what are built on a solid foundation;" a question arose in my mind, what foundation I had to hope for heaven? I examined and found I had none but what was built on the sand, and at death I must fall into hell; which caused a cry to be started from my heart to my maker, what I should do? a thought passed through my mind to make a resolution to amend my way, and turn and be good, but a second thought came powerfully into my mind, if I made another resolution and broke it as I had done, the door of mercy would be forever shut against me. Then the good spirit brought to my mind the dangers and deaths from which I had been delivered, through the mercy of an indulgent God, and how I had called on him in trouble and he delivered me, and had answered me in the secret place of thunder; and it was pressed on my mind, that it was too dangerous to make another fool's start: then I seemed to be in the wilderness, not knowing what to do: a thought arose in my mind, you have got into a pretty fix now, afraid even to make a resolution of amendment; then an enquiry again arose in my heart, from that depth of thought, what I should do? at the same time the hand-writing of God appeared against me, and that power that once shook the earth, shook my soul and body: it pressed on my mind, that it was the great power of

God: and that word came into my mind, "they that resist shall receive to themselves damnation;" at the same time, the spirit of truth brought all things to my remembrance, my sins old and new, little and big, and I saw how hateful they all were in the sight of a holy God. Now let the Lord be praised both now and forever, for the exceeding riches of his grace to all who will look at their sins, and his goodness, and consider and think, before it be too late, and be sorry, and turn from the evil of their ways, that they may understand the truth.

And now, reader, attend to the word sent to me in my distress, which was this "believe on the name of the Lord Jesus Christ, and thou shalt be saved." Oh! then, and not till then, did I ever desire saving faith; but I could not attain to it by all the exertion I could make but Oh! reader, I found here in my distress, that faith is the gift of God, and that grace is not sown in the heart, till the heart is broken and contrite: that is, in earnest to study and enter into the saving plan of life and salvation, which is: "Let the wicked forsake his way, and the unrighteous man his thoughts, and let them turn unto the Lord, and he will have mercy upon him, and abundantly pardon all that is passed." But when I was put to the test to try my faith, I found I had none: then in the bitterness of my spirit, I desired the Lord to give me to feel the power of saving faith; and I struggled to lay hold on that word, "Ask and ye shall receive, seek and ye shall find;" but a question made me quake--which question was this: is your heart right? then I trembled, but could not tell whether my heart was right or not; and while I desired to know myself, this form passed through my mind; "Are you willing now to renounce the devil and all his works, and all the pomp and vanity of this wicked world, and all the sinful lusts of the flesh;" and I was enabled in my sinking, distressed state, to forsake every forbidden way for the sake of peace and pardon.--Then did God send down the power of saving faith; then, Oh! how terrible I saw the length, and breadth, and depth, and height of God's eternal law: I also saw that heaven and earth would pass away, before one jot or tittle of his law should fail, or fall to the ground. Man must be converted, or never enter into the kingdom of heaven. A thought came into my heart, to go out to some secret place to pray; and as I walked I trembled, and when I got to the place, I could only pray, "Lord have mercy upon me." I cried as if falling into black despair, and having consented to forsake every wrong way, God, for Christ's sake, had mercy on me, and pardoned my sins: Glory be to God, for ever and ever, Amen. Oh! praise the Lord, whose mercy is over all his works, from generation to generation, who hath put down the mighty from their seats, and hath exalted them of low degree, and ever holds his servant Israel in remembrance of his mercy. Oh!

how faithful and true he is, to all who will yield to the striving of his spirit in their own hearts, before it takes its everlasting flight. Oh! how careful ought we to be, for fear we be left to ourselves; then blindness of mind, and hardness of heart will take place, and the soul be left to stumble on the dark mountains of unbelief, on which many have stumbled since the world began for not following the light that visits their mind; which appeareth in youth, and continueth with some shorter, and some longer, according to the entertainment this heavenly messenger gets in the hearts of all people. Oh! reader, think how many are now in the road to ruin, who are still slighting the call of grace; and if they keep on, must overtake them that are there already; and now I pray that none that sees this, may ever go another step towards the pit, from whence there is no return.

"Oh! that all may taste and see

The riches of his grace:
"The arms of love that compass me,
"Would all mankind embrace!"

Having given the reader a short account of the abundant mercy bestowed on me by a bountiful God, who is engaged to raise poor sinners from a depth of sin and shame, to the height of happiness and glory; and if they yield to him he will do it, for faithful is he that has called you, who also will do it, if ye be willing and obedient. I now return to give the reader an account of the difficulties I met with, in buying my wife.

She was born a slave, and continued a slave till she was about thirty-two years of age, and I about twenty-eight years old; and having paid for myself, and got a little money beforehand, I was provoked to purpose buying of her. Before this, she and her master had fallen out, and he purposed to send her, and our first daughter, about three months old, away to the back countries; and how to do I did not know: to go with her I knew not where, or buy her at his price, brought me to a stand: and while I was perplexed, there came a messenger to me, who said her master had carried the negro buyer with him from court, in order to sell her to him; but when they were about to count out the money, his daughter broke out and cried in such a distressing manner, for my little daughter, that it caused him to recant at that time; but he made two more attempts, but was mis-put most providentially. At the same time, her master and I were both on one class-paper, which made it very trying to me, to keep up true love and unity between him and me, in the sight of God: this was a cause of wrestling in my mind; but that scripture abode with me, "He that loveth father or mother, wife or children, more than me, is not worthy of me;" then I saw it became me to hate the sin with all my heart, but still the sinner love: but I should have fainted, if I had not looked to Jesus, the author of my faith: but I would remark, that at the very moment I was about to give up, the Lord appeared for my help, to my great surprise. It pleased almighty goodness, to give my wife's mistress that power which cut Rahab and wounded the Dragon; and she spoke with such concern of mind and said, "Oh do let Solomon have her; I have been afraid to speak, but I want him to have her, he appears to want to have her;" and these words, with a few more I omit, were attended with such force to her master's mind, that he gave up with a whining tone, and said "He may have her;" so I hired her, and took her away the same day. After the year was out I went to pay him his money for her hire, and it being on a meeting day, some friends there who saw me pay the money, said to me, "you had better buy your wife at once;" her master answered, "I want him to buy her:" then they insisted on knowing his price; he said, "a hundred dollars, and give in all the hire;" which was fifty dollars less than ever he had mentioned before: I then said I would undertake it then they insisted we should have it in writing and we had it so. Thus I entered purchase of my wife, one hundred and three dollars and a third, which is thirty one pounds Virginia money. When the articles were drawn I desired the writer to put down what was paid, and what was due; and then went on working and paying, until I had paid all but forty dollars and four pence.

But here I will mention a remarkable circumstance: I grew uneasy about my wife and me living together without being married; and while I was studying how to bring it about, a tradition arose in the Methodist church, to turn out all [illegible] members, that lived together as man and wife without being married: at the same time, preaching being held at her master's house the day came round for meeting; after public meeting, the class was called, when to my great surprise, the preacher asked me if I was free? I answered "yes:" he asked "if I had a wife?" I said "yes:" he asked, "are you married?" I answered "no:" he asked "if my wife was free?" I said "no, not properly so:" he asked "who had any claim on her?" the class leader said "Brother Melson:" the preacher asked me "if I was willing to be married" I answered "yes," and added, "I had been concerned about it, but did not know how to bring it to pass:" the preacher said, "it is easy driving when we are willing;" and then, before the society, added his reason as above, and said, "I suppose Brother Melson will have no objection." Melson, her master, answered, "they may be married, and welcome, for what I care:" then said the preacher, "you can just give him an instrument to the clerk of the court, and he can get a license and be married, and finish your business afterwards:" he then wrote to the same effect, and I went and got a license, and we were married according to law.

Now the reader may take notice, that when we bargained, her master agreed to free her upon my paying him his money, or give me a bill of sale to empower me to free her; but after I had paid him about sixty-three dollars, he then took pet, and said "he would take her away, without I paid him all," which was forty dollars and four-pence due: now he had given me receipts for all the money I had paid him, but no bill of sale or freedom. By this time my wife had one child after we bargained: he said he "would have the negroes or money;" but we being married, according to law, it made her mine; and the Judge of the court told me, "that her master could not get her, nor any more money:" but I felt easiest to do according to bargain, if he would fulfill according to agreement: but it was with great difficulty I got him to fix the business; when done, then I paid him, and then she was manumitted free, and I desired rest.

But I had one child in bondage, my only son, my first-born son; and having worked through the purchase of myself and wife; I thought I would give up my son, to the ordering of divine providence. So we worked on and got to farming, and were favored, so that we did not fall through in twelve or thirteen years, renting land, and paying up, and keeping clear of the world.

Now the reader may take notice, that as I was going on thus, my son's master died; and his property had to be sold, and my son had to be sold, as the other property, at public sale: the back-woods-men being come over, and giving such large prices for slaves, it occasioned a great concern to come over my mind; and I began to tell my concern to some friends, white and cultured, rich and poor; and they all with one accord persuaded me to buy him, that is, my son: I answered I could have no heart, because he was appraised at the death of his master at four hundred dollars; it being the latter end of the war in America, 1813, and the times dark and dull, I was much afraid to attempt to buy him: but I told my friends what was like to befell me, that when my son was nine months old, then I was sent away from him, as I told the reader in the beginning of my journal, and then I went through a fit of distress, and now he is like to be sent away from me, and then I shall have to go through another fit, and it will seem like double trouble but my friends and neighbors continued pressing it on me, to meet the day of sale, and buy him; and finally I concluded to do it, and met the day of sale.

Then the crier made a noise in the court yard, before the court house door, and said, "a likely young negro fellow for sale," and then asked for a bid; the second time he asked for a bid, I bid two hundred dollars, which was half what he was appraised to, at the death of his master. As soon as ever I had bid two hundred dollars, the man, I feared would buy and sell him to the back-country men, bid three hundred and thirty three dollars and a third, which was thirty-three dollars and a third more than I had intended to bid, which beat down all my courage. But a thought struck me, don't give out so, so don't; so I bid a shilling: then the same man bid twenty dollars, which was three hundred and fifty-four dollars: at that I sighed, and thought I must give him up, and let him go; but a thought came into my mind, to bid one time more, and not bid any more, if he went to the West Indies: so I bid a cent; but the crier said, no Solomon, not a cent, a shilling: well says I, let it go. As soon as my bid was confirmed, the same man went on, and I gave up then. My son had chosen a master, a justice of peace in town, said to be a good master, who had promised me before the sale began, that if he saw me give up, he would try and buy him; so he began and moved him up to three hundred and fifty-seven dollars, then he gave up. Then three great men, who had agreed to be my securities, were standing by; one of them was a Methodist preacher, very rich; he looked at me as if he pitied me, and when he saw my son was likely to go off the wrong way, he says, "three shillings;" and when he spoke I cried, and turned off, and went and leaned against the court house, under a weight of concern; and as I was considering, that word came into my mind, "this is their hour and the power of darkness," so I gave him up then. Now it did appear, the very moment I gave him up, and hope left me, then help came; for it pleased the

Most High, who pitied every sorrowful soul, in the riches of his mercy, to look on two young men that were acquainted with me, and to touch their hearts, with such a sense of sympathy and pity towards my case, that they could not endure; and the dear young neighbor man, a great man's son, says to my young master, who were both standing in the ring looking on, he says, "I had rather give twenty dollars out of my own pocket, than Solomon should not get him, but if Solomon will bid once more, I will give him four dollars:" my young master answered, "if you will give him five dollars, I will give him five dollars," and says, "let us go and tell him," so they both came to me, as I was learning against the court house wall, and said in a moving tone, "Solomon, if you will bid one more bid, we will give you five dollars apiece;" I turned round and says, "a shilling," which was a shilling upon three hundred and sixty dollars. Then a great man said, "there, let the old man have him, he is his son, he wants him, he can get security:" so they kept at that till the switch went down; so he was knocked off to me at three hundred and sixty dollars and a shilling. Then the tender-hearted young man, that first proposed to my young master, went into the store, and brought five round silver dollars, and gave to me in the office, where I went to sign the bond; then three of my securities agreed upon the spot, to make me up twenty dollars at the day of payment.

By this time I got raised up from my sadness, and went out after I had signed the bond, so much revived and clothed with such a spirit of faith and courage, believing a way would be opened for me to get through, though I could not tell how; but as I came out of the office, I met the executor and administrator who said to me, "well, Solomon, you have got Spence after all;" I said, "yes, master George, but I gave up, and if it had not been for those men who pitied me, and who did as they did, I never should have got him, and now what will you give me?" He put his hand into his pocket, and pulled out a round silver dollar and gave me, which caused me to rejoice more for that one dollar, than for the twenty dollars promised me just before in the office: and now I will give the reader my reason why I rejoiced more for the one than for the twenty dollars; because two days before the sale, he, the executor and administrator, offered a challenge to me and to them I trusted in, touching the sale of my son; now as he was the first that put me in heart to try to buy my son, I thought it right, two days before the sale, to go to him and hear what he had to say to me; and when I got there, he says, "well Solomon, where are you going?" I said, "I am come down to meet the day of sale;" he said, "well, what are you going to do?" I answered, I want to buy my son if I can; he says, "you do?" and added, "you will have a hard time of it;" I answered, "I have been thinking so;" he says,

"Solomon, there are four men who say they will give four hundred dollars for your son;" then says I "they will get him;" he says, "Solomon what are you willing to give?" I answered, "not more than two hundred and fifty dollars;" he says, "you will not get him for that, but I suppose you are so much in favor with the people,

nobody will bid against you; but if nobody will bid against you, I will; you need not think you are going to get him for nothing," and he seemed angry; then I was very sad at that saying, and says, "master George, you was the very first man that put me in heart, and now you seem to put me out of heart; "then he, in an angry gust of manner, said, "well Solomon, try your faith, and added, you remember the birds, and how you exercised faith, and was delivered; now try your faith;" as though he felt as if he could defy the armies of the living God: but when he gave me the dollar, then I thought of the challenge "now try your faith." I then believed, that God could work and none could hinder him: although it appeared this man had done what he could, to bring me into that difficulty, yet, when through the goodness of the Highest I was encouraged, as above described, and being brought down as it were to nothing before the Lord, I was enabled to ask him in such a way that his hand and heart appeared to be opened, so that he gave me that dollar, for which I rejoiced more than for the twenty dollars promised me just before, as above stated: then was I enabled to sing aloud the praises of our king in spirit and in truth, whoever sits above, till all his foes submit and bow to his command, and fall beneath his feet: I confess the eyes of my mind appeared to be dazzled, as I was let into a sight of the great goodness of the Highest in undertaking for me: but Oh! reader, I felt a fear, lest my behavior should not be suitable to the kindness and favor shewed towards me.

Now there was an impression on my mind, that the Father of Mercy would do greater things for me, for his own honor and praise, and my everlasting advantage, if my behavior was right before him: it was impressed on my mind, that he was unchangeable in his purposes and designs, which are to set the captive souls at liberty, if they will follow him in the path of obedience; and no degrees of grace will destroy man's capability of choosing, whether he will do right or wrong; doing right gives a secret satisfaction to the mind; but doing wrong is followed by a secret uneasiness, because God will be a swift witness against the wrong, and will justify what is right in man's words and deeds, when done with right views. Oh! that all men would study the end of their creation, and act accordingly; then they would walk in the light of his countenance indeed, and "in his name they would rejoice all the day, and in his righteousness for ever be exalted;"

"Then should their sun in smiles decline,
"And bring a peaceful night;"
which, may all who read these lines, desire, seek, and obtain, through Jesus Christ our Lord Amen, and Amen.

EXTRACT OF A LETTER TO R. H.;

dated, Cambden, 1st of 2nd month, 1824.

"ESTEEMED FRIEND,

I received thy*

* The reader will observe, that Solomon frequently makes use of the pronoun "thee," when addressing an individual; this occurs simply from the circumstance, that it is a mode of speech not unusual in some parts of America, with people of different denominations; and does not arise from any connexion that he has ever had with the society of friends.

R. H.

book and pens, with a letter unsealed, yesterday, dated 1st month, 17th, 1824, requesting some account of my deceased mother and daughters. Dear Robert, thy letter discovered a sign of generosity, or concern, for the good of all people; and this concern enables thee to be condescending to men of low estate; wherefore I pray, that the condescending grace of God, that has begun with thee, may continue with thee, all the days of thy life; and that through the all-sufficient merits of Christ, both thee and thy family, all may be brought to Sion's hill; and that you may be enabled to join the blessed company, to sing redeeming love, for ever and ever, Amen.

"If thou go home to England, then I shall see thee no more; but I trust to see you in the land of rest, where partings are no more, * * * * * the grace of our Lord Jesus Christ, be with your spirits. Amen:

"SOLOMON BAYLEY."

I now proceed to give some brief account of the nativity, life, and death, of my mother. She was born of a Guinea Woman, who was brought from Guinea about the year 1690, as near as I can guess; and said to be about eleven years old when brought to America. But oh! how different is the situation of things, towards the cultured people since that day; the Lord certainly is at work in the rising generations, to have more pity and compassion than in ages past. My Grandmother was bought into one of the most barbarous families of that day; and although treated hard, was said to have fifteen sons and daughters: she lived to a great age, until she appeared weary of life.

My mother had thirteen sons and daughters; she served the same cruel family, until they died. Then great distress and dispersion took place: our young mistress married, and brought our family, out of the state of Virginia, into the state of Delaware. After some years, her husband removed back into Virginia: after that law took place against moving slaves, which entitled all of us to freedom; we made a move to recover it by that law; but we soon were all sold and scattered very wide apart, some to the east, and some west, north, and south. My father and mother they pretended to set free, to stop a trial in court, and after they had been free about eleven months, they came upon them unawares; my father Abner, sister Margaret, and brother Abner, were taken in the night, and carried to Long Island, one of the West India Islands, and sold to Abner Stephen; he has sent two letters here, or we never should have known what had become of them.

On the same night as above cited, my mother being in the house, they meant to take her; but she made an excuse to go out at the door, and ran and left her sucking child, and her two other children, and her husband my father: now it being winter time, the child cried; they therefore left it and carried away my father and the other two children. Then some friend took the child and carried it to mother; then mother took her son about eleven months old, and travelled near a hundred miles from the State of Virginia to Dover in Kent County, State of Delaware; and from thence to New Jersey.

In this time she testified she experienced great affliction both of body and mind; but at length, like Hagar, she was enabled to see Him who had seen her in all her affliction, and not only to see him in the works of creation, but also in the works of his providence; and her mind was enlightened to see into the nature and largeness of her sins. She also testified, that the view of eternity and of eternal consequences, so distressed her mind, that it swallowed up her present distress, and so she was induced to give up the lesser, and attend to the greater; namely, to find peace and rest in the life to come: she was enabled to go on in search after truth, until she experienced peace of mind, and evidence of pardon for all her sins, which was her greatest concern till death.

Now the number of years that we were parted, mother and I, was about eighteen; except that once in a great hurry. I travelled more than a hundred miles to see her; at the same time I left keeping of a saw mill, my wife, and young child about a month old, and taking with me seventeen or eighteen dollars, which all because a sacrifice with my time, to the relief of my mother; but I was favored to find that satisfaction, which I esteemed more than time or money.

Now it came to pass after eighteen years, my mind was visited with a concern to go to Africa after that Paul Cuffee had been there, and brought good tidings from that place;-*

* This concern was doubtless of a religious character: the death of the pious and enterprising Paul Cuffee, was the probable canse of the visit being relinquished.
R H.

therefore I thought it good to put out my children in good families, where they could get some schooling, and learn how to work, and then get my wife in with some good sort of people; and being advised to wait till it should seem proper to recommend me to that service, I thought it right to engage in some profitable business, and was hired to attend a mill, in which time the case of my mother came before me, and I sent for her to the State of Delaware from New Jersey; and when brought together, it was indeed like heaven on earth begun; we could sit and tell of the dangers and difficulties we had been brought through; so my mother was favored to end her days with me: she, like my grandmother lived to a great age and appeared weary of affliction, and of this troublesome world; her mind became disordered; she desired a short illness, which was granted; she died the third day after she was taken sick, with very little complaint or struggle; but was thought to have fallen asleep.

A BRIEF ACCOUNT OF MY ELDEST DAUGHTER, MARGARET BAYLEY,
Who died in the twenty-fourth year of her age.

She was a pleasant child in her manners and behavior, yet fond of gay dress and new fashions; yet her mind was much inclined to her book, and to read good lessons.

And it pleased the Father of mercy to open her understanding, to see excellent things out of his law, and to convince her that it was his will she should be holy here and happy hereafter; but custom, habit, and shame, seemed to chain her down, so that she appeared like one that was halting between two opinions.

But about a month before she was taken for death, she went to Meeting under a concern about her future state; and the Meeting appeared to be favored with the out pouring of the spirit of love, and of power: Margaret came home under great concern of mind, and manifested a wonderful change in her manners and behavior; I believe the whole family were affected at the sight of the alteration, which indeed appeared like that of the prodigal son coming home to his father; for my own part I felt fear and great joy; such was her delight to read the Bible, and ask the meaning of certain texts of Scripture, which evidenced a concern to make sure work for eternity.

In this frame of mind she was taken for death; she appeared very desirous to live for the first four weeks, but was very patient, and of a sweet temper and disposition all the time: I recollect but one instance when she was known to give way to peevish fretfulness; then I, feeling the evil spirit striving to get the advantage of her, very tenderly and earnestly admonished her not to regard trifles, but to look to that power which was able to save her; and from that time she became passive and resigned.

The following two weeks her pain was great, and baffled all the force of medicine: a few days before her departure, she was urged with much brokenness of heart to make confession; when she was let into a view of the vanity of the world, with all its glittering snares; and said, she could not rest till her hair was cut off; for she said, "I was persuaded to plait my hair against my father's advice, and I used to tie up my head when father would come to see me, and hide ruffles and gay dress from him, and now I cannot rest till my hair is cut off." I said, "no, my daughter, let it be till thee gets well:" she answered, "Oh! no, cut it now:" so I to pacify her took and cropped it.

After this she appeared filled with raptures of joy, and talked of going, as if death had lost its sting; this was about three days before her departure; she seemed to have her senses as long as she could speak: a little before her speech left her, she called us all, one by one, held out her hand, bade us farewell, and looked as if she felt that assurance and peace that destroyed the fear of death; and while she held out her hands, she earnestly charged us to meet her in heaven.

Thus ends the account of Margaret Bayley, daughter of Solomon and Thamar Bayley, who departed this life the 26th of the 3rd month, 1821, aged twenty-three years, eleven months, and twenty-eight days.

TO THE PIOUS READER.

I desire to give the pious, a brief account of the life and death of my youngest daughter, Leah Bayley, who departed this life the 27th of the 7th month, 1821, *aged twenty-one years, six months, and one day.*

She, from a child, was more weak and sickly than her sister Margaret, and the thought of leaving her here in this ill-natured world caused me many serious moments; but the great Parent of all good, in the greatness of his care, took her away, and relieved me of the care of her for ever.

Weakness of body and mind appeared in her as she grew up; and an inclination to vanity and idleness; but being bound out under an industrious mistress, to learn to work and to have schooling, her mind soon became much inclined to her book and then to business. Her school mistress gave her a little book, concerning some pious young people that lived happily and died happily, and were gone to heaven namely,

Young Samuel, that little child, Who served the Lord, liv'd undefiled. Like young Abijah I must be, That good things may be found in me. Young Timothy, that blessed youth, Who sought the Lord and loved the truth.

I must not sin as others do
Lest I lie down in sorrow too.

These blessed examples won her heart, so as to bury every other enjoyment: she seemed to possess as great a deadness to the world, as any young woman I ever observed: she seemed not ashamed to read in any company, white or cultured; and she read to the sick with intense desire, which appeared from her weeping, and solid manner of behavior. She seemed to desire to walk in the fear of the Lord all the day long: everybody that observed her, remarked her serious steady behavior; she seemed as if she was trying to imitate those good children whom she read about; and so continued until she was taken sick;

and although her sickness was long and sharp, yet she bore it like a lamb.

A few days before her decease, I was noticing how hard she drew her breath: she looked very wistful at me, and said, "O! father, how much I do suffer:" I answered, "yes, my dear, I believe thee does:" then, after a long pause, she said, "but I think I never shall say I suffer too much:" this I apprehend was extorted from a view of the sufferings of Christ, and her own imperfections this was about three days before her decease. The day she died, she called us all, one by one, and like her sister Margaret, held out her hand, and with much composure of mind bade us farewell, as if she was only going a short walk, and to return.

EXTRACT OF A LETTER TO R. H.

Dated 3rd month 26th, 1824.

"I thank thee, dear Robert, for spending a thought on so poor and unworthy a thing as I am; but I especially thank your God and my God, for putting it into thy heart to enquire anything about the work of grace on my mind. I trust it is with gratitude I now write unto thee of my call to the ministry: and first I may say,

"God works in a mysterious way," "His wonders to perform."

Secondly, he knows how to get himself honor and praise by the most feeble; for to undertake to make such a creature as I am, work in his vineyard, was amazing to me; but there was a great work to do, to make me fit for anything at all; surely he called me oftener than he did Samuel, when he was a child: but after I was savingly converted to God, he was pleased to pour into my heart a measure of his universal love; and when my heart was filled with love towards God, and good will towards all mankind; then a longing desire that all people might taste and see the riches of his grace, continued with me day and night; then a strong impression to go in the fear of the Lord and speak to men of all descriptions, seemed to be required of me.

But Oh! dear friend, after my mind was thus prepared, I had a great warfare and strife; first, with man-fear, and a man-pleasing spirit, then with shame, desire of praise, and a good name.

Now, dear friend, in this exercise of mind there were some scriptures came into my mind, to encourage and strengthen me; such as, the II. Corinthians, xii. 9--II. Kings, v. 4--I.

Corinthians, i. 21, 27, 28, and chapter xi. 3. also chapter ix. 16, 22--II. Corinthians, xi, 29--Daniel xii. 3--Isaiah vi. 5--Jeremiah i. 6--John i. 15, and chapter iii. 2--Hebrews xi. 34; all these scriptures mightily helped to encourage me to go forward in speaking to a dying people, the words of eternal life. Oh! what an affecting view of the worth of souls, came into my mind; and I thought, if I could be made instrumental in the hand of the Lord, in saving one soul, it would be matter of rejoicing to all eternity. So I went out trusting in the Lord; but I should soon have fainted in mind, if it had not been for the encouragement I met with, both from God and man. Now to Him that sits upon the throne be honor and praise, world without end. Amen.

"With good wishes to thee and thine, I conclude, thy friend,

"SOLOMON BAYLEY"

YOUNGMAN, PRINTER, WITHAM AND MALDON.